J.K. Rowling

ABDO
Publishing Company

Buddy BOOKS
First Biographies

by
Sarah Tieck

VISIT US AT
www.abdopublishing.com

Published by ABDO Publishing Company, 8000 West 78th Street, Edina, Minnesota 55439.

Printed in the United States of America, North Mankato, Minnesota.
092009
012010

 PRINTED ON RECYCLED PAPER

Coordinating Series Editor: Rochelle Baltzer
Contributing Editors: Heidi M.D. Elston, Megan M. Gunderson, BreAnn Rumsch, Marcia Zappa
Graphic Design: Jane Halbert
Cover Photograph: *Getty Images*: DAVID CHESKIN/AFP
Interior Photographs/Illustrations: *AP Photo*: Evan Agostini (p. 19), Bonhams, PA (p. 15), Jennifer Graylock (p. 29), Suzanne Mapes (p. 7), Lefteris Pitarakis (p. 17), Lisa Poole (p. 11), Bizuayehu Tesfaye (p. 19), Kirsty Wigglesworth, file (pp. 24, 25) Press Association via AP Images (p. 27); *Getty Images*: MARCUS BRANDT/AFP (p. 23), Fred Duval/FilmMagic (p. 20), Eamonn McCormack/WireImage (p. 5); *iStockphoto.com*: ©iStockphoto.com/ ChrisHepburn (p. 13), ©iStockphoto.com/jvoisey (p. 9).

Library of Congress Cataloging-in-Publication Data

Tieck, Sarah, 1976-
  J.K. Rowling / Sarah Tieck.
    p. cm. -- (First biographies)
  ISBN 978-1-60453-987-5
  1. Rowling, J. K.--Juvenile literature. 2. Authors, English--20th century--Biography--Juvenile literature. I. Title.
  PR6068.093Z8886 2010
  823'.914--dc22
  [B]
                              2009032374

Table of Contents

Who Is J.K. Rowling?

J.K. Rowling is a famous British author. She is known for writing the seven-book Harry Potter **series**.

The Harry Potter books have sold more than 300 million copies! They have helped many people become interested in reading. Some say the stories teach people life lessons, too.

J.K. and her character Harry Potter have the same birthday!

J.K.'s Family

J.K. Rowling is the writing name of Joanne "Jo" Rowling. J.K. was born on July 31, 1965, near Bristol, England. She was the first child of Anne and Pete Rowling. J.K. has one younger sister named Dianne.

When J.K. was young, the Rowlings moved to Winterbourne, England. Later, J.K. would use memories of this town and its people in her writing.

J.K.'s publisher wanted her to change her name. So, she used her grandmother's name, Kathleen, to make the writing name J.K.

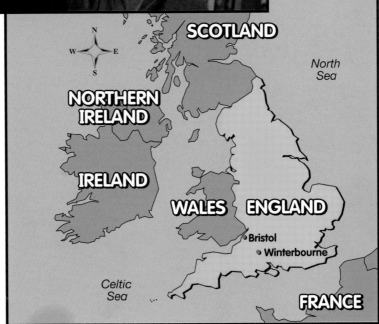

SCOTLAND

North Sea

NORTHERN IRELAND

IRELAND

WALES ENGLAND

Bristol
Winterbourne

Celtic Sea

FRANCE

Growing Up

Even as a child, J.K. loved to write stories. She wrote her first story when she was about six. It was about Rabbit and his friend Miss Bee.

When J.K. was nine, her family moved to a village near Chepstow, Wales. This area had a big forest. J.K. loved to play in the trees. The forest sparked her imagination.

Many of Harry Potter's adventures take place in forests.

SCOTLAND

North Sea

NORTHERN IRELAND

IRELAND

WALES

ENGLAND

Chepstow

Celtic Sea

FRANCE

When J.K. was 15, she learned her mother had **multiple sclerosis (MS)**. As her mother grew sicker, J.K. became sad. Later, J.K. would use her feelings and experiences in her books.

After high school, J.K. attended the University of Exeter in southern England. There, she studied French. J.K. **graduated** in 1986.

Several well-known universities honored J.K. after she became an author. One was Harvard University in the United States.

Family Troubles

In 1990, J.K. got an idea for a story. Soon, she began to write about a boy **wizard** named Harry Potter.

That same year, J.K.'s mother died. J.K. became very sad. In 1991, she moved to Portugal to teach English. There, she got married. In 1993, her daughter Jessica was born.

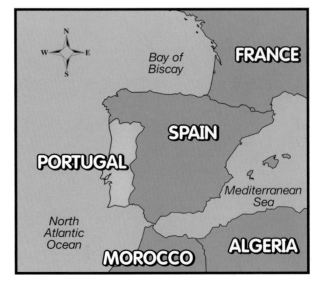

Shortly after, J.K. and Jessica moved to Edinburgh, Scotland. J.K. divorced her husband. She and Jessica were very poor. But, J.K. worked hard. She cared for Jessica and kept writing.

Edinburgh, Scotland

The First Book

In 1998, *Harry Potter and the Sorcerer's Stone* was **published** in the United States. It is about a boy who learns he is a **wizard**. He has many adventures while attending a school for wizards.

The book quickly grew popular with children and adults. J.K. was excited about the book's success. It helped her make a better life for herself and Jessica.

HARRY
POTTER
and the Philosopher's Stone

J.K.ROWLING

9¾

HOGWARTS EXPRESS

"A terrific read and

J.K.'s book was first published in England in 1997. There, it was called *Harry Potter and the Philosopher's Stone*.

A Growing Family

In 2001, J.K. married a doctor named Neil Murray. They had two children. Their son, David, was born in 2003. Their daughter, Mackenzie, was born in 2005. Today, J.K. and her family live in Scotland.

J.K.'s husband Neil (*right*) and her friends call her Jo.

Famous Author

Over the next ten years, J.K. **published** six more Harry Potter books. The books follow Harry's life as he studies magic and battles evil.

Fans loved Harry. They also loved his friends Ron and Hermione. The **fantasy** book **series** became so popular it was printed in more than 60 languages! And, the books were made into movies.

British actor Daniel Radcliffe plays Harry in the Harry Potter movies.

Some fans have collected all the books in the series.

Sometimes, J.K. feels shy. She says it can be hard to be so well known.

The Harry Potter books changed J.K.'s life. She is often **interviewed** for magazines and television. People take her picture. And, fans wait in long lines to meet her.

J.K. loves her fans, but she protects her private life. She doesn't like it when strangers take pictures of her family. She wants her family to have a normal life.

The Last Book

Harry Potter and the Deathly Hallows was **published** in 2007. It is the seventh and last book in the **series**. In this book, Harry faces his enemy, Lord Voldemort.

People were very excited for the last Harry Potter book. It was **released** at midnight. Some people waited at bookstores to get their copy. There were parties to celebrate.

Many fans wore costumes for the release of *Harry Potter and the Deathly Hallows*.

J.K. attended an event to celebrate the **release** of her final Harry Potter book. It was held at the Natural History Museum in London, England. There, J.K. read to 500 fans and signed 1,700 books!

J.K.'s publisher had a drawing to choose who would attend her reading. Around 90,000 fans entered the drawing.

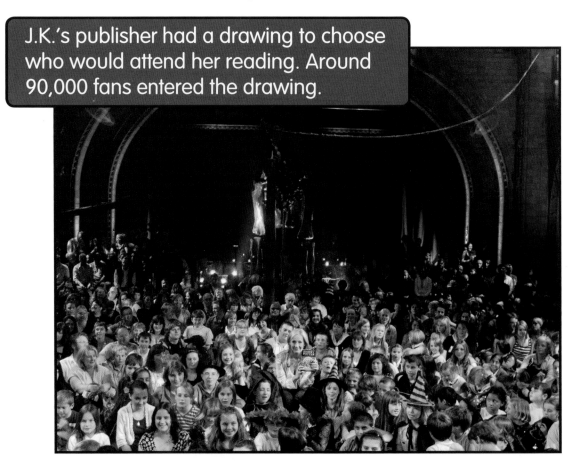

Harry Potter book covers look different in other countries.

Free Time

When J.K. isn't writing, she spends time with her family and friends. She likes to shop for shoes and bake cakes.

In addition, J.K. enjoys helping people. In 2002, she started a **charity**. J.K. also gives money to help fight against **MS**.

To raise money for children, J.K. handwrote and illustrated a special book. It sold for almost $4 million!

Future Plans

J.K. doesn't plan to write more Harry Potter books. She is at work on a fairy tale for children. She doesn't know when it will be **released**. For now, J.K. Rowling says she is just enjoying writing.

J.K.'s Harry Potter books continue to gain fans.

Important Dates

1965 J.K. Rowling is born on July 31. Her real name is Joanne "Jo" Rowling.

1986 J.K. graduates from the University of Exeter.

1990 J.K. gets an idea for a book about a boy wizard. J.K.'s mother dies.

1991 J.K. moves to Portugal to teach English.

1993 J.K.'s daughter Jessica is born. J.K. and Jessica move to Edinburgh, Scotland.

1998 The first Harry Potter book is published in the United States.

2001 J.K. marries Neil Murray. They later have a son, David, and a daughter, Mackenzie.

2007 The last Harry Potter book is published.

Important Words

charity a group or fund that helps people in need.

fantasy (FAN-tuh-see) a type of story that uses magic and made-up elements.

graduate (GRA-juh-wayt) to complete a level of schooling.

interview to ask someone a series of questions.

multiple sclerosis (MS) (MUHL-tuh-puhl skluh-ROH-suhs) a disease that affects a person's brain and spine. It can cause speech problems and a loss of muscle control.

publish to print the work of an author.

release to make available to the public.

series a set of similar things or events in order.

wizard a person who is skilled in magic.

Web Sites

To learn more about J.K. Rowling, visit ABDO Publishing Company online. Web sites about J.K. Rowling are featured on our Book Links page. These links are routinely monitored and updated to provide the most current information available.

www.abdopublishing.com

Index